Instant OSSEC Host-based Intrusion Detection

A hands-on guide exploring OSSEC HIDS for operational and security awareness

Brad Lhotsky

[PACKT]
PUBLISHING

BIRMINGHAM - MUMBAI

Instant OSSEC Host-based Intrusion Detection

Copyright © 2013 Packt Publishing

All rights reserved. No part of this book may be reproduced, stored in a retrieval system, or transmitted in any form or by any means, without the prior written permission of the publisher, except in the case of brief quotations embedded in critical articles or reviews.

Every effort has been made in the preparation of this book to ensure the accuracy of the information presented. However, the information contained in this book is sold without warranty, either express or implied. Neither the author, nor Packt Publishing, and its dealers and distributors will be held liable for any damages caused or alleged to be caused directly or indirectly by this book.

Packt Publishing has endeavored to provide trademark information about all of the companies and products mentioned in this book by the appropriate use of capitals. However, Packt Publishing cannot guarantee the accuracy of this information.

First published: July 2013

Production Reference: 2160813

Published by Packt Publishing Ltd.
Livery Place
35 Livery Street
Birmingham B3 2PB, UK.

ISBN 978-1-78216-764-8

www.packtpub.com

Credits

Author
Brad Lhotsky

Reviewers
JB Cheng
Scott Miller
Mark Stanislav

Acquisition Editor
Mary Nadar

Commissioning Editor
Meeta Rajani

Technical Editor
Hardik B. Soni

Copy Editors
Insiya Morbiwala
Gladson Monteiro

Project Coordinator
Esha Thakker

Proofreader
Lindsey Thomas

Graphics
Ronak Dhruv

Production Coordinator
Nilesh R. Mohite

Cover Work
Nilesh R. Mohite

Cover Image
Ronak Dhruv

About the Author

Brad Lhotsky started working with Unix systems professionally in 1998 as a system administrator, database administrator, network engineer, programmer, and security administrator. He has been an active member of the OSSEC HIDS community since 2004. He currently administers one of the largest OSSEC HIDS deployments in the world!

> First, I'd like to thank my beautiful wife, April, for inspiring and supporting me in everything I do.
>
> Thanks also to Clinton, Tim, Wouter, and Willem for their helpful suggestions.

About the Reviewers

JB Cheng has over 20 years' experience in the networking and security industry. His professional experiences include working for the IBM RTP Network Management Division, AT&T Wireless Data Division, and WatchGuard Unified Threat Management appliance development group. Since 2007, he has joined Trend Micro as a Senior Staff Engineer and is currently the OSSEC project manager responsible for OSSEC releases and for engaging with the open source community. His personal blog can be found at http://ossec-notebook.blogspot.com/.

> I would like to thank Daniel Cid for creating OSSEC and making it an open source project. Without him you wouldn't be reading this book today, period.

Scott Miller is a Linux administrator, security professional, and IT professional in Raleigh, North Carolina. His expertise includes system administration, Apache/nginx, Amazon web services, security, and Linux. He has worked in large-scale academia IT environments as well as in the enterprise private sector in mission-critical environments. Currently employed at MetaMetrics, Inc. in Durham, NC, he has previously worked for Qualys, UC Davis, and UC Berkeley. Scott is a contributor to many online IT blogs and outlets.

Mark Stanislav is the security evangelist for Duo Security, an Ann Arbor, Michigan-based start-up focused on two-factor authentication and mobile security. With a career spanning a decade, he has worked within small businesses, academia, start-up, and corporate environments primarily focused on Linux architecture, information security, and web application development. He holds a Bachelor's degree in Networking and IT Administration and a Master's in Technology Studies focused on Information Assurance, both from Eastern Michigan University. He also holds his CISSP, Security+, Linux+, and CCSK certifications.

www.PacktPub.com

Support files, eBooks, discount offers and more

You might want to visit www.PacktPub.com for support files and downloads related to your book.

Did you know that Packt offers eBook versions of every book published, with PDF and ePub files available? You can upgrade to the eBook version at www.PacktPub.com and as a print book customer, you are entitled to a discount on the eBook copy. Get in touch with us at service@packtpub.com for more details.

At www.PacktPub.com, you can also read a collection of free technical articles, sign up for a range of free newsletters and receive exclusive discounts and offers on Packt books and eBooks.

PACKTLIB

http://PacktLib.PacktPub.com

Do you need instant solutions to your IT questions? PacktLib is Packt's online digital book library. Here, you can access, read and search across Packt's entire library of books.

Why Subscribe?

- Fully searchable across every book published by Packt
- Copy and paste, print and bookmark content
- On demand and accessible via web browser

Free Access for Packt account holders

If you have an account with Packt at www.PacktPub.com, you can use this to access PacktLib today and view nine entirely free books. Simply use your login credentials for immediate access.

Table of Contents

Preface — 1
Instant OSSEC Host-based Intrusion Detection — 7
  Installing OSSEC (Simple) — 7
  Configuring an OSSEC server (Simple) — 12
  Getting agents to communicate (Simple) — 14
  Writing your own rules (Simple) — 17
  Detecting SSH brute-force attacks (Intermediate) — 23
  Configuring the alerts (Simple) — 28
  File integrity monitoring (Simple) — 32
  Monitoring command output (Intermediate) — 35
  Detecting rootkits and anomalies (Simple) — 39
  Introducing active response (Intermediate) — 42
  Verifying alerts with active response (Advanced) — 45

Preface

Welcome to *Instant OSSEC Host-based Intrusion Detection*. We're going to jump into exploring the vast possibilities that OSSEC HIDS offers its users. We'll dive into the installation and basic configuration of OSSEC HIDS so you can start protecting your valuable assets today! From there, we will build on these basic concepts to explore harnessing the power of OSSEC HIDS's flexible decoders, rules, and active responses to unlock powerful, time-saving functionality. We will challenge the notion that security software will slow you down and create more work by leveraging OSSEC HIDS's automation capabilities to do our work so we can spend more time at the pub!

What this book covers

Installing OSSEC (Simple) gets you started with installing OSSEC HIDS through a few different methods. We look at both source and binary installs to get OSSEC HIDS installed and ready to configure.

Configuring an OSSEC server (Simple) takes you through the basic configuration of the OSSEC HIDS server. This server allows us to perform aggregations and correlations across our install base to make better decisions.

Getting agents to communicate (Simple) walks us through the basics of setting up our OSSEC HIDS agents to communicate with the OSSEC HIDS server. We also look at utilizing the OSSEC HIDS authentication daemon to make this process simpler for larger installs.

Writing your own rules (Simple) asks you to roll up your sleeves and start extending the OSSEC HIDS rules to better suit your environment. We look at the ossec-logtest tool to understand how our rules are being interpreted.

Detecting SSH brute-force attacks (Intermediate) takes a look at the compound rules of OSSEC to see how we can detect events based on their frequency. We also delve into the decoders that make compound rules possible!

Preface

Configuring the alerts (Simple) looks at various options for adjusting the alert volume for OSSEC HIDS. We start with some broad, sweeping approaches to decrease e-mails and gradually increase our granularity. We also explore the different channels for alerting.

File integrity monitoring (Simple) briefly explains what FIM is and why it's useful for product security. After that, we dissect the problem and tune our alerting to more useful levels so we don't trip over the number of alerts!

Monitoring command output (Intermediate) demonstrates a few operational intelligence capabilities of OSSEC HIDS through the monitoring of the command output. We will look into monitoring the command output either line by line or all at once.

Detecting rootkits and anomalies (Simple) looks at the rootkit and policy auditing of OSSEC HIDS. We look at some of the possible problems with these modules and how we can solve them without compromising our coverage.

Introducing active response (Intermediate) walks us through the configuration and use of OSSEC HIDS active response systems to execute scripts in response to alerts. We'll block IP addresses attempting to perform a brute-force login attack over SSH.

Verifying alerts with active response (Advanced) delivers the promise of this book. We look at how to use the entire OSSEC HIDS framework to get our computers to work for us. Slaving through false-positive alerts is not the job of a security administrator, so we'll put OSSEC HIDS to work!

What you need for this book

The concepts in this book should be generic enough to cover OSSEC HIDS on any operating system it supports, including Linux, BSD, Solaris, HP-UX, and Microsoft Windows. The author's primary experience is with Linux systems, so some of the examples may bias towards that environment.

This book is not a manual page and is not sentient. It cannot respond to voice commands and textual inquiry (yet!). Where should you turn when you have problems that have not been covered in this book? There are plenty of resources available online to assist you in configuring OSSEC HIDS.

Official documentation

The first place to start is the official documentation that is available online at `http://www.ossec.net/?page_id=11`. Linked from the site, you'll find the Reference Manual, FAQ, installation guides and videos, and tutorials written by OSSEC community members. Everything from starting a simple standalone installation through to writing your own decoders and rules is covered in depth on the site.

The community

OSSEC HIDS has a vibrant community of developers and users who make themselves available through a number of channels. Depending on your preferred method of communication, you can find help on IRC (Internet Relay Chat) or through the OSSEC users' mailing list.

The mailing list is a great resource as many of the questions OSSEC users might ask are likely to have been asked and answered in great depth on the mailing list. The list is hosted on Google Groups, which makes searching the archive pleasant and useful. You can find the mailing list at the following link:

```
https://groups.google.com/forum/?fromgroups#!forum/ossec-list
```

If you're familiar with IRC, you can find a group of OSSEC users and developers hanging out in #ossec on irc.freenode.net. IRC is a great way to consult OSSEC gurus on topics such as "Where do I look for X" or "Is Y even possible?" (spoiler: yes it is). To find out more about how to connect to FreeNode, see the documentation at the following link:

```
http://freenode.net/faq.shtml#usingfreenode
```

Even if you don't have a question, subscribe to the mailing list and/or hang out on IRC. If you have OSSEC HIDS running on your network, chances are you might be able to help someone else get it up and running. You don't need to be a developer to help keep the community vibrant and alive!

Commercial support

Trend Micro, who owns OSSEC HIDS, provides commercial support contracts. While not preferred by the author, some organizations require commercial support contracts for the software they deploy on critical infrastructure. Management, who prefer to avoid open source software, may find comfort with OSSEC as they can have a professional services contract with Trend Micro to maintain the OSSEC architecture in the event that the original administrator(s) leaves the company. This eliminates the "bus factor" normally associated with deploying open source solutions.

Who this book is for

This book is great for everyone who is concerned about the security of their servers but assumes some knowledge of basic security concepts and rudimentary scripting experience. Whether you are a system administrator, programmer, or security analyst, this book will provide you with tips to better utilize OSSEC HIDS. Whether you're new to OSSEC HIDS or a seasoned veteran, you'll find something in this book that you can apply today!

Conventions

In this book, you will find a number of styles of text that distinguish between different kinds of information. Here are some examples of these styles, and an explanation of their meaning.

Code words in text, database table names, folder names, filenames, file extensions, pathnames, dummy URLs, user input, and Twitter handles are shown as follows: "Binary installers will label their server packages as `ossec-hids-server`."

A block of code is set as follows:

```
<global>
  <email_notification>yes</email_notification>
  <email_to>security.alerts@example.com</email_to>
  <smtp_server>localhost</smtp_server>
  <email_from>ossecm@server.example.com</email_from>
</global>
```

When we wish to draw your attention to a particular part of a code block, the relevant lines or items are set in bold:

```
<syslog_output>
  <level>10</level>
  <server>critical-events.example.com</server>
  <port>514</port>
  <format>json</format>
</syslog_output>
```

Any command-line input or output is written as follows:

```
$ sudo apt-get install ossec-hids-server
```

New terms and **important words** are shown in bold. Words that you see on the screen, in menus or dialog boxes for example, appear in the text like this: "OSSEC provides a binary installer for Windows on the **Downloads** page of the site."

Reader feedback

Feedback from our readers is always welcome. Let us know what you think about this book—what you liked or may have disliked. Reader feedback is important for us to develop titles that you really get the most out of.

To send us general feedback, simply send an e-mail to `feedback@packtpub.com`, and mention the book title via the subject of your message.

If there is a topic that you have expertise in and you are interested in either writing or contributing to a book, see our author guide on `www.packtpub.com/authors`.

Customer support

Now that you are the proud owner of a Packt book, we have a number of things to help you to get the most from your purchase.

Downloading the example code

You can download the example code files for all Packt books you have purchased from your account at http://www.packtpub.com. If you purchased this book elsewhere, you can visit http://www.packtpub.com/support and register to have the files e-mailed directly to you.

Errata

Although we have taken every care to ensure the accuracy of our content, mistakes do happen. If you find a mistake in one of our books—maybe a mistake in the text or the code—we would be grateful if you would report this to us. By doing so, you can save other readers from frustration and help us improve subsequent versions of this book. If you find any errata, please report them by visiting http://www.packtpub.com/submit-errata, selecting your book, clicking on the **errata submission form** link, and entering the details of your errata. Once your errata are verified, your submission will be accepted and the errata will be uploaded on our website, or added to any list of existing errata, under the Errata section of that title. Any existing errata can be viewed by selecting your title from http://www.packtpub.com/support.

Piracy

Piracy of copyright material on the Internet is an ongoing problem across all media. At Packt, we take the protection of our copyright and licenses very seriously. If you come across any illegal copies of our works, in any form, on the Internet, please provide us with the location address or website name immediately so that we can pursue a remedy.

Please contact us at copyright@packtpub.com with a link to the suspected pirated material.

We appreciate your help in protecting our authors, and our ability to bring you valuable content.

Questions

You can contact us at questions@packtpub.com if you are having a problem with any aspect of the book, and we will do our best to address it.

Instant OSSEC Host-based Intrusion Detection

Welcome to *Instant OSSEC Host-based Intrusion Detection*. This book will walk you through the installation, configuration, and customization of the OSSEC **host-based intrusion detection system** (**HIDS**). We will explore many features of OSSEC and how they can be used to improve the overall security, provide valuable insight into systems operations, automate the detection of false positives to provide relevant alerting data, and more.

Installing OSSEC (Simple)

In this chapter we'll download, install, and configure a simple OSSEC local profile. This profile incorporates all of the OSSEC's features into a single installation that will work on its own. OSSEC also supports a server-agent model, where a dedicated server profile provides aggregation and analysis for every agent profile.

Instant OSSEC Host-based Intrusion Detection

Getting ready

So, what is it we're getting ourselves into? OSSEC is an acronym for **Open Source SECurity Event Correlator**. OSSEC monitors systems for events in logfiles and processes on the filesystem through the use of commands and outputs. It decodes the data, extracting valuable information, and analyzes it in context.

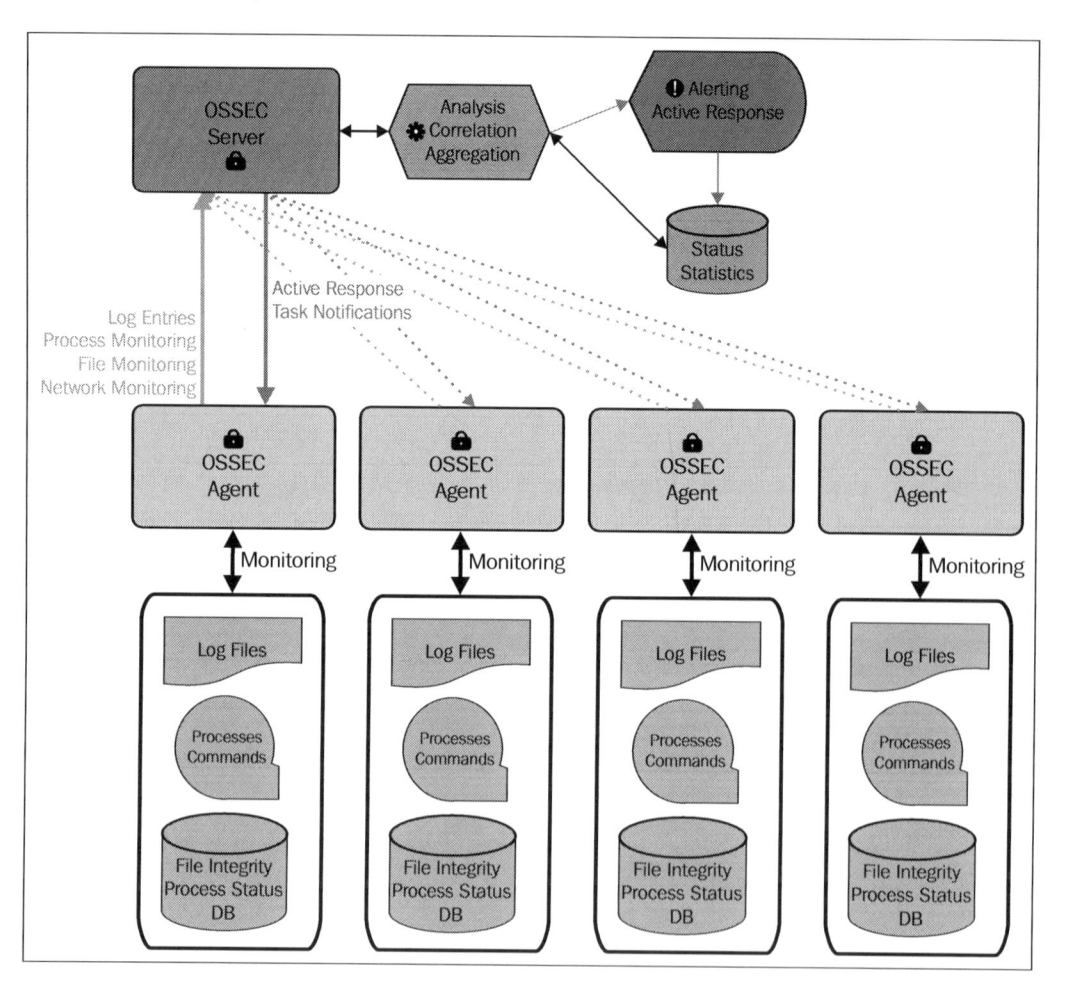

As the previous diagram shows, the analysis and correlation is used to generate alerts, either e-mails or logs, or active responses. **Active response** is a simple framework for running a script or program within the context of the alert. Using active response, we can call a firewall script with the source IP that just failed to log in to our server via SSH.

The functionality of the local profile is identical to that of the server-agent model, except all components function locally. Let's start out with a simple local profile installation.

To install OSSEC from source, you will need only a C compiler available on the system and the superuser access. OSSEC does not require any external libraries and builds its own self-contained binaries to avoid corruption or deception should your server be compromised.

Generally, most Linux/BSD operating systems ship with or have a C compiler available. It's usually the GNU C compiler (GCC). If GCC isn't already installed, you can simply consult your system's package manager to install it on any Linux- or BSD-based systems.

Now the only thing left to prepare is downloading and extracting the source tarball. You can retrieve the proper archive file from `http://www.ossec.net/?page_id=19`. Download the latest stable release, extract it, and change its directory into the folder created for extracting the archive.

How to do it...

OSSEC developers provide a wrapper script to encapsulate the configure, build, and install process into a single, prompted installation. The installation is guided, but we can look at a few important prompts along the way:

1. To get started, run the installation script with superuser privileges as follows:

   ```
   $ sudo ./install.sh
   ```

   The first important question is what type of installation we will be performing:

   ```
   1- What kind of installation do you want (server, agent, local, hybrid or help)?
   ```

   The simplest configuration is the `local` profile. This configures OSSEC as a standalone daemon analyzing and correlating only locally to this system. It's a good starting point to get familiar with OSSEC.

2. After a few simple questions, check for a prompt asking which analyzers to enable:

   ```
   3.2- Do you want to run the integrity check daemon? (y/n) [y]:
   ```

   The integrity check daemon monitors your critical files and binaries for changes. This is usually referred to as **file integrity monitoring** or **FIM**.

   ```
   3.3- Do you want to run the rootkit detection engine? (y/n) [y]:
   ```

   The rootkit detection engine is a combination of signature- and anomaly-based checks to discover the presence of popular or yet-to-be-discovered rootkits on Linux/BSD systems. It looks for out-of-place or hidden files and strange-network behavior.

   ```
   3.4- Do you want to enable active response? (y/n) [y]:
   ```

Active response provides a functionality to run scripts when alerts are triggered. This feature provides the capacity for OSSEC to move beyond a detection system into a prevention system. There are a few tested responses that come standard with OSSEC.

```
- Do you want to enable the firewall-drop response? (y/n) [y]:
```

If you have an active response enabled, OSSEC ships with a firewall-drop response that works on almost every operating system, without modification, and creates a firewall rule to drop traffic coming from IPs identified by the rules as attackers.

```
- Do you want to add more IPs to the white list? (y/n)? [n]:
```

If you have the firewall-drop response enabled, you'll be prompted to create a whitelist of IPs that will never be blocked by the active response system. If you have networks or IPs that you'd prefer not to be blocked, you can configure them here. Generally, critical systems should be excluded: DNS servers, LDAP servers, and mail servers. Without this protection, OSSEC may interrupt key communication channels during an attack. If you selected yes, use spaces to separate IPs and/or networks in CIDR notation, for example:

```
- IPs (space separated):
  192.168.0.0/23 10.0.0.0/8 1.2.3.4
```

OSSEC will now be built based on your answers to questions and information attained through the build tools on your system. If everything goes successfully, the last message you see should look something similar to the following:

```
Installation Completed.
```

If you don't see this message, check the error message and correct the issue. OSSEC is designed to build without external libraries but failures will occur if there's no C compiler found.

How it works...

So, what just happened? There's a lot of output, so let's cover the highlights. The script configures and builds the OSSEC binaries. Once the compilation has completed, the OSSEC users and groups are created on the system if they do not exist. The OSSEC installation directory is created, and the binaries and configuration files we complied are copied into their permanent location on the filesystem. The script then verifies and repairs permissions in the OSSEC installation directory to ensure a working installation. If everything completes successfully, the last step starts the OSSEC daemons and begins analyzing your logs.

It's important that system administrators are aware of the user and group creation as they might be utilizing configuration management software and may wish to create the users and groups prior to running the installation script. The users created are:

- `ossec`: This is the default OSSEC user
- `ossecm`: This is the OSSEC mailer daemon
- `ossecr`: This is the OSSEC remote daemon

A single group named `ossec` containing all these users is also created.

The end result of the process is a default configuration of OSSEC. By now, OSSEC is already gathering log data and analyzing your filesystem.

There's more...

Congratulations! You just installed, configured, and started OSSEC to protect your server. An excellent first step in the mastery of OSSEC! You might also be thinking that there is a lot of work to run this setup process on each server, and you're right. It's not always desirable or possible to perform source installs on every server in your network. Luckily for us, there's a speedier way!

Binary installations

On most production systems, a C compiler may not available. Don't worry, it is still possible to deploy it on these systems without requiring administrators to install hefty development packages.

OSSEC provides a binary installer for Windows on the **Downloads** page (http://www.ossec.net/?page_id=19) of the site. This is an agent-only binary, so you will still require a Linux/BSD server to manage any Windows agents.

For Linux systems, there are two major package managers, **RPM** and **APT**. Distributions based on Red Hat use a binary package called an RPM. Atomicorp provides a handy installer for their nicely packaged OSSEC RPMs, which you can install using the following command on your Red Hat server:

```
$ wget -q -O - https://www.atomicorp.com/installers/atomic |sudo sh
```

After that, you'll be able to install the OSSEC server or agent through `yum`:

```
$ sudo yum install ossec-hids-server
```

Or for a client install, use the following command:

```
$ sudo yum install ossec-hids-client
```

Instant OSSEC Host-based Intrusion Detection

If you intend to install it on a Debian-based Linux distribution, *Nicolas Zin* has packaged OSSEC for Ubuntu. His work is available at the following link:

`https://launchpad.net/~nicolas-zin/+archive/ossec-ubuntu`

Follow his instructions to enable the source in APT. Install OSSEC server by running the following command:

`$ sudo apt-get install ossec-hids-server`

Or for a client install, use the following command:

`$ sudo apt-get install ossec-hids-agent`

Integrating the deployment of OSSEC into your organization's configuration management solution is much easier with binary packaging. Servers receiving a binary package do not require a C compiler to be installed. This often fits within the organization's requirements to remove unnecessary software from its infrastructure.

Starting OSSEC at boot

Even though OSSEC may already be running, we need to make sure that we configure our installation to start during the operating system's boot sequence. This step varies depending on the operating system you're running. The easiest way to start OSSEC on Linux/BSD is to add the `/var/ossec/bin/ossec-control start` command to the `/etc/rc.d/rc.local` file, which is executed at boot.

If you've chosen the binary package install, chances are that the package provides an initialization script for your operating system. Most modern systems use an initialization script usually installed as `/etc/init.d/ossec-hids`, and the following commands will enable it:

- Red Hat-based: `/sbin/chkconfig ossec-hids on`
- Debian-based: `/sbin/update-rc.d ossec-hids defaults`

The Microsoft Windows binary installer configures OSSEC to run at startup, so no additional steps are necessary.

Configuring an OSSEC server (Simple)

The standalone or local configuration is perfect for managing a single server. If you have multiple servers, you'll want to use OSSEC in the server-agent model. Utilizing a server-agent model will allow agents to aggregate events and the server to make more informed decisions when alerting or taking an action.

Getting ready

In this example, we assume that the:

- OSSEC server is 192.168.0.1
- Our servers live on 192.168.0.0/23 (192.168.0.1 to 192.168.1.254)
- We have an external MS Exchange server at 1.2.3.4

We also assume that you have successfully installed OSSEC. Otherwise, you can install it from the source or with a binary installer. To install from a source, use the `install.sh` command and select `server` as the installation type in the first step. Binary installers will label their server packages as `ossec-hids-server`.

In order to run OSSEC in server mode, you need to open up the UDP port 1514 on your firewalls from and to your OSSEC server.

How to do it...

Now that the server is ready, we'll have to double-check the remote namespace in the `/var/ossec/etc/ossec.conf` file:

1. To configure the remote daemon and to communicate with them, we just need to make sure that we implement the following configuration:

```
<remote>
    <connection>secure</connection>
    <allowed-ips>192.168.0.0/23</allowed-ips>
</remote>
```

2. Another key setting in server mode is the whitelist for active response. Set it up now as illustrated in the following configuration, even if you don't plan on utilizing the active response:

```
<global>
  <!--Our LAN -->
  <white_list>192.168.0.0/23</white_list>
  <!-- MS Exchange Server -->
  <white_list>1.2.3.4</white_list>
</global>
```

3. We will then verify and configure our e-mail settings as follows:

```
<global>
  <email_notification>yes</email_notification>
  <email_to>security.alerts@example.com</email_to>
  <smtp_server>localhost</smtp_server>
  <email_from>ossecm@server.example.com</email_from>
</global>
```

4. We can then establish our basic e-mail and log thresholds as follows:

   ```
   <alerts>
     <log_alert_level>1</log_alert_level>
     <email_alert_level>7</email_alert_level>
   </alerts>
   ```

5. Don't forget to restart the server for the changes to take effect:

   ```
   $ sudo /var/ossec/bin/ossec-control restart
   ```

How it works...

The simple configuration options we've specified for our server simply enable the secure communication over the UDP port 1514 between OSSEC clients and the server. We also configured the server to accept connections from our internal networks.

The best practice is to whitelist any IP addresses of potential agents as well as any known external business-critical resources. By whitelisting critical resources, we can ensure that OSSEC never interrupts service to those resources. Any resource that is critical in an emergency should be whitelisted, which is why we have whitelisted the external mail server.

Imagine being under attack and suddenly losing access to e-mail! The last two blocks configure OSSEC to send an e-mail on our network. If we need a specific SMTP server, we can tweak it here. Once we have our e-mail configured, we establish the thresholds for alerting at events whose level is 7 or higher. We will log any events whose level is 1 or higher.

Getting agents to communicate (Simple)

Now that the server has been configured, this recipe covers how one can configure the clients to connect to the server to increase the intelligence and relevance of alerts.

Getting ready

In this example, we assume that the:

- OSSEC server is 192.168.0.1
- Our servers live on 192.168.0.0/23 (192.168.0.1 to 192.168.1.254)

We also assume that you have successfully installed OSSEC. You can install it from the source or with a binary installer. To install from a source, use the `install.sh` command and select `agent` as the installation type in the first step. Binary installers will label their agent packages as either `agent` or `client`. The Debian package is labeled `ossec-hids-agent` and the Red Hat package is labeled `ossec-hids-client`.

If you're using a binary package, the `ossec.conf` file will need to be updated. We need to point the OSSEC agent process to the correct server. For our example network, we'd modify the `/var/ossec/etc/ossec.conf` file to have its `client` section look similar to the following:

```
<client>
    <server-ip>192.168.0.1</server-ip>
</client>
```

The only other thing we need to do is to set up the client and server keys.

How to do it...

If you were to start OSSEC at this point, the `ossec-agentd` component would fail to start while the rest of the components would function. This is because you have not told the OSSEC server about the existence of this new agent. To do that, we need to create keys and import them on the client:

1. On the server, perform the following:

   ```
   $ sudo /var/ossec/bin/manage_agents
   *****************************************
   * OSSEC HIDS v2.7.1 Agent manager.       *
   * The following options are available:   *
   *****************************************
          (A)dd an agent (A).
          (E)xtract key for an agent (E).
          (L)ist already added agents (L).
          (R)emove an agent (R).
          (Q)uit.
   Choose your action: A,E,L,R or Q:
   ```

2. Select A to add an agent. You will be prompted for that agent's fully qualified domain name and IP address. Once you've confirmed adding the agent, you'll receive the menu again. This time, you need to extract the agent key for importing the client, so select E and enter the ID of the agent you just created. You'll be presented with an output that looks similar to the following:

   ```
   Agent key information for '001' is:

   MDAxIHNlcnZlci51eGFtcGxlLm51dCAxOTIuMTY4LjAuMTUyIDgyZTZjNjI1ZDQ2Zm
   I2MD1kYTFmMDkxNDA2NTYwNTU2YWQyZGZhMTBmZGYwMGJlODcwNTAxYTcxNDY
   5MWMxMmY=
   ```

3. The agent key is Base64 encoded and in this case starts with `MDAx`. Copy that key to your clipboard; on the client, run the `manage_client` script to import it:

   ```
   $ sudo /var/ossec/bin/manage_client
   ****************************************
   * OSSEC HIDS v2.7.1 Agent manager.     *
   * The following options are available: *
   ****************************************
        (I)mport key from the server (I).
        (Q)uit.
   Choose your action: I or Q:
   ```

4. Choose `I` to import the key and paste the Base64-encoded string into the prompt. You should now see the key information decoded as:

   ```
   Agent information:
      ID:001
      Name:server.example.net
      IP Address:192.168.0.152
   ```

5. If everything looks correct, press *Y* to import the key. At this point, the client and server are aware of each other, and you may start (or restart) OSSEC on the client as follows:

   ```
   $ sudo /var/ossec/bin/ossec-control restart
   ```

How it works...

This process creates the shared secret key between the OSSEC server and the client. With this key, and a combination of the ID and IP of the client, messages may pass safely between the server and client. This ensures that the commands coming in over UDP are legitimate commands from the server and not an attacker masquerading as the OSSEC server.

The `/var/ossec/etc/client.keys` key file on the OSSEC server should be considered sensitive and any unauthorized access to it should prompt serious actions, such as resetting the keys on all the clients. The `client.keys` file should be as restricted as possible on every system to prevent tampering. The default permissions allow only the group `ossec` to read the file.

There's more...

Key management can slow down the automated deployments. Luckily, OSSEC fixed this in the version 2.5 with the introduction of the authentication daemon.

Managing agent keys automatically

The manual key setup process is burdensome, especially if you'd like to deploy to hundreds or thousands of servers. To fix this, the `ossec-authd` file was introduced to provide a mechanism for an agent to request a key if one does not exist.

On the server, `/var/ossec/bin/ossec-authd` is installed with the server profile. And on the client, `/var/ossec/bin/agent-auth` is installed as a part of the agent profile.

The `ossec-authd` file is a simple daemon that has a single configurable option and the port to use, which is specified on the command line via the `-p` option (the default is 1515):

```
$ sudo /var/ossec/bin/ossec-authd -p 1515
```

You may also need to create the SSL keys for `ossec-authd`. To do so:

```
$ openssl genrsa -out /var/ossec/etc/sslmanager.key 2048
$ openssl req -new -x509 -key /var/ossec/etc/sslmanager.key \
          -out /var/ossec/etc/sslmanager.cert -days 365
```

On the client, we use the `agent-auth` command to request a key from the OSSEC server. The `-m` option manages the keys and the OSSEC server in our example. The `-A` option is the agent name, which defaults to the hostname (as does our example):

```
$ sudo /var/ossec/bin/agent-auth -m 192.168.0.1 -A $(hostname)
```

If this is successful, you should be able to view the contents of the client file:

```
$ sudo cat /var/ossec/etc/client.keys
```

> **Downloading the example code**
>
> You can download the example code files for all Packt books you have purchased from your account at `http://www.packtpub.com`. If you purchased this book elsewhere, you can visit `http://www.packtpub.com/support` and register to have the files e-mailed directly to you.

Writing your own rules (Simple)

So we have a running OSSEC server. It's configured to send us e-mails with alerts and we're getting a lot of e-mails. Not every alert is actionable or interesting in our environment. We can fine-tune alerts by overriding, supplementing, and enhancing the base rule set with our `rules/local_rules.xml` file.

By leveraging OSSEC's rules, we can tune rules based on the username, IP address, source hostname, URL, filename, time of the day, day of the week, rules matched, frequency, and time since last alert. The rules provide a powerful way to tweak the alerts we receive and are a great starting point for customization as no coding is required.

Instant OSSEC Host-based Intrusion Detection

Getting ready

Before we start writing rules, we should be aware of some rules to be followed:

- The **first rule** of writing custom rules is to never modify the existing rule files in the `/var/ossec/rules` directory except `local_rules.xml`. Changes to those rules may modify the behavior of entire chains of rules and complicate troubleshooting.

- The **second rule** of writing custom rules is to use IDs above `100000` as IDs below it are reserved. Interfering with those IDs is the same as tampering with the distributed rules files themselves. You risk an update of OSSEC clobbering all your hard work.

- The **third rule** is to maintain order in your rules. As the rules parser is loading the rules at startup, it validates the existence of referenced rules and groups. If you reference a rule that hasn't been loaded, the parser will fail.

Minding these three rules helps to ensure that our installations won't break with upgrades and that we can always get back to a "stock" OSSEC by removing the `local_rules.xml` file from our configuration.

Every rule must have an ID, a level, a description, and a match condition. The IDs must be unique, and our rules must have an ID over `100000`. It's important to note that re-using or reordering rule IDs can cause confusion or inaccuracy in historic data.

Rules in OSSEC have a level from 0 to 15. The higher the level, more certain the analyzer is of an attack. Level 0 is a special level to tell OSSEC to ignore the alerts where no log will be generated and OSSEC will discard the alert and data silently. By default, OSSEC considers anything at or exceeding level 7 to be e-mail worthy, but it is also configurable.

Rules also require a `description` field to explain what the rule does. This description will be used as the event identifier in the e-mails and log messages that OSSEC generates. As it will be a part of the reporting, it's best to explain the rule professionally and format it consistently. Descriptions like "alerting for this thing" won't be helpful to your colleagues, whereas "Ignore failed login attempts from vulnerability scanners between 4:00 and 7:00" will be clear and informative.

Now that we're well versed with the protocols of the rules, let's process some data from our custom application logging via syslog as follows:

```
May 4 19:12:03 server custom-app: Startup initiated.
May 4 19:12:07 server custom-app: No error detected during startup!
May 4 19:12:08 server custom-app: Startup completed, processing data.
May 4 19:12:08 server custom-app: Failed login from '4.5.6.7' as testuser
```

We're receiving an alert about unknown errors and authentication failures from our custom application. We would prefer to silence these unknown error messages and ensure that we don't provide alerts for failed logins from `4.5.6.7`, our vulnerability scanner.

How to do it...

In order to figure out the first step, we need to understand what's happening to generate the alerts:

1. Use the `ossec-logtest` tool provided by OSSEC. It works by accepting log messages on `STDIN` (your terminal input) and explaining the path through the rules. Here's how we can run it:

   ```
   $ sudo /var/ossec/bin/ossec-logtest
   ```

2. Then we can paste in log lines to see which ones are generating alerts:

   ```
   ossec-testrule: Type one log per line.

   May  4 19:12:03 server custom-app: Startup initiated.

   **Phase 1: Completed pre-decoding.
          full event: 'May  4 19:12:03 server custom-app: Startup initiated.'
          hostname: 'server'
          program_name: 'custom-app'
          log: 'Startup initiated.'

   **Phase 2: Completed decoding.
          No decoder matched.
   ```

3. The first log message completed the parsing of the line and no alert was generated. So we try the next log message:

   ```
   **Phase 1: Completed pre-decoding.
          full event: 'May  4 19:12:07 server custom-app: No error detected during startup!'
          hostname: 'server'
          program_name: 'custom-app'
          log: 'No error detected during startup!'

   **Phase 2: Completed decoding.
          No decoder matched.

   **Phase 3: Completed filtering (rules).
          Rule id: '1002'
          Level: '2'
          Description: 'Unknown problem somewhere in the system.'
   **Alert to be generated.
   ```

4. We can see from this output that our *unknown problem* is being generated by this log line. We get the rule ID and the level being generated and using this information, we can write a rule to ignore it using OSSEC's `level="0"`.

   ```
   <!-- Local Rules for Example.com -->
   <group name="local,syslog,">
      <rule id="100000" level="0">
        <if_sid>1002</if_sid>
        <program_name>custom-app</program_name>
        <description>Ignore errors for custom-app</description>
      </rule>
   </group>
   ```

5. Once we've saved the `local_rules.xml` file, we can restart `ossec-logtest` and try the event again:

   ```
   **Phase 3: Completed filtering (rules).
       Rule id: '100000'
       Level: '0'
       Description: 'Ignore unknown errors for custom-app'
   ```

6. Now that we've moved this event to level 0, we can look at the failed login events:

   ```
   May  4 19:12:08 server custom-app: Failed login from '4.5.6.7' as testuser'
   **Phase 3: Completed filtering (rules).
       Rule id: '2501'
       Level: '5'
       Description: 'User authentication failure.'
   **Alert to be generated.
   ```

7. We'll use a simple match with this data to silence this alert from 4.5.6.7:

   ```
   <rule id="100001" level="0">
     <if_sid>2501</if_sid>
     <program_name>custom-app</program_name>
     <match>4.5.6.7</match>
     <description>Ignore failed logins from scanner</description>
   </rule>
   ```

8. And now re-running `ossec-logtest`, we see:

   ```
   May  4 19:12:08 server custom-app: Failed login from '4.5.6.7' as testuser'

   **Phase 3: Completed filtering (rules).
       Rule id: '100001'
       Level: '1'
       Description: 'Ignore failed logins from our security scanner'
   **Alert to be generated.
   ```

Using these two rules, we've been able to silence the noisiest log entries in our sample environment.

How it works...

OSSEC rules are processed sequentially. Each rule has a number of conditions and a logical AND is applied to the conditions. The more specific we make the rule, the more accurate it will be. In our example, we filtered events using the `program_name` attribute for the string, `custom-app`.

Each rule also specifies an `if_sid` element, which requires the log message to be flagged with the rule ID we specify. The `if_sid` parameter can take a comma-separated list of rule IDs, where the rule will match if any of those IDs are matched. Consider that multiple instances of the same element appear in a rule; refer to the following example:

```
<match>illegal user</match>
<match>unknown user</match>
<match>invalid user</match>
```

That grouping is surrounded in logical OR. It's important to note that after our rules match, the ID is changed and other rules looking for those lines with the same `if_sid` parameter, which was originally set, will fail to match. When a new rule matches, it replaces the attributes of the alert with its own values, replacing the ID and level.

While our first rule stopped at eliminating the match based on the rule ID and program name only, the second rule used the `match` attribute to find a string in the log message itself. In addition to `match`, there is also a `regex` attribute to allow more flexible matching of strings.

To see a complete list of fields available, check out the OSSEC documentation on rules' syntax available at the following link:

```
http://www.ossec.net/doc/syntax/head_rules.html
```

Instant OSSEC Host-based Intrusion Detection

There's more...

OSSEC rules are quite capable. We saw how to modify an alert based on the `if_sid` parameter, which is the rule ID. We saw that we can adjust the rule level using the level of the new rule. Most cases will involve this type of rule-level promotion or demotion depending on the context. We can evaluate events based on a number of fields. We used `ossec-logtest` to see some of those fields, but we're missing data. In our examples, we saw the following message:

```
**Phase 2: Completed decoding.
       No decoder matched.
```

Without a decoder, our event data is limited to simple string matches. Let's take a look at what decoders are and how they work.

Decoding event data

Our custom application does not have a valid decoder because we didn't build one. Not every program needs a decoder and we were able to be effective without it. Decoders provide a way to extract field data from the message to be used in context, but not every rule needs a decoder. We saw some of these fields in the pre-decoding phase where common data are extracted:

```
**Phase 1: Completed pre-decoding.
       full event: 'May  4 19:12:08 server custom-app: Failed login from '1.2.3.4' as testuser''
       hostname: 'server'
       program_name: 'custom-app'
       log: 'Failed login from '1.2.3.4' as 'testuser'
```

In our rule, we even used the `program_name` attribute to match our custom application from the log stream.

OSSEC ships with an array of decoders out of the box, consider the output of this default install using `ossec-logtest` to read an SSH log message:

```
May  4 19:11:01 ether sshd[3747]: Accepted publickey for brad from 1.2.3.4 port 48801 ssh2


**Phase 1: Completed pre-decoding.
       full event: 'May  4 19:11:01 ether sshd[3747]: Accepted publickey for brad from 1.2.3.4 port 48801 ssh2'
       hostname: 'ether'
       program_name: 'sshd'
       log: 'Accepted publickey for brad from 1.2.3.4 port 48801 ssh2'
```

```
**Phase 2: Completed decoding.
    decoder: 'sshd'
    dstuser: 'brad'
    srcip: '1.2.3.4'

**Phase 3: Completed filtering (rules).
    Rule id: '5715'
    Level: '3'
    Description: 'SSHD authentication success.'
**Alert to be generated.
```

To learn more about decoders, including writing custom decoders, refer to the OSSEC documentation on decoders:

`http://www.ossec.net/doc/manual/rules-decoders/create-custom.html`

Detecting SSH brute-force attacks (Intermediate)

The rules engine tracks its state; it knows what's been happening in the recent past. We can leverage that information to alert or squelch alarms based on frequency of events. The most common example of this is to detect and defend against SSH brute-force password attacks.

Getting ready

This is such a common problem the SSH brute-force detection and active response is built into OSSEC and enabled by default. We're going to take a look at the rules that interact to provide this functionality and provide an explanation of those rules. This will give us insight into how to write something similar for a web application log.

How to do it...

The decoder provides the analyzer with interesting elements out of the log messages, normally using regular expressions. Like the rules engine, the decoder is extensible and configurable. We can easily add decoders for our in-house application logs using the same techniques.

1. Let's look at a decoder to extract the user and source IP from SSHD log messages involving login failures.

The following snippet comes from OSSEC's default decoders in
`/var/ossec/etc/decoders.xml`:

```
<decoder name="sshd">
  <program_name>^sshd</program_name>
</decoder>

<decoder name="ssh-invfailed">
  <parent>sshd</parent>
  <prematch>^Failed \S+ for invalid user|^Failed \S+ for illegal
user</prematch>
  <regex offset="after_prematch">from (\S+) port \d+ \w+$</regex>
  <order>srcip</order>
</decoder>

<decoder name="ssh-failed">
  <parent>sshd</parent>
  <prematch>^Failed \S+ </prematch>
  <regex offset="after_prematch">^for (\S+) from (\S+) port \d+ \
w+$</regex>
  <order>user, srcip</order>
</decoder>

<decoder name="ssh-error">
  <parent>sshd</parent>
  <prematch>^error: PAM: Authentication \w+ </prematch>
  <regex offset="after_prematch">^for (\S+) from (\S+)$</regex>
  <order>user, srcip</order>
</decoder>
```

The following rules were selected from the distribution's `rules/sshd_rules.xml` file:

```
<rule id="5700" level="0" noalert="1">
  <decoded_as>sshd</decoded_as>
  <description>SSHD messages grouped.</description>
</rule>

<rule id="5716" level="5">
  <if_sid>5700</if_sid>
  <match>^Failed|^error: PAM: Authentication</match>
  <description>SSHD authentication failed.</description>
  <group>authentication_failed,</group>
</rule>

<rule id="5720" level="10" frequency="6">
  <if_matched_sid>5716</if_matched_sid>
  <same_source_ip />
```

```
    <description>Multiple SSHD authentication failures.</
description>
    <group>authentication_failures,</group>
</rule>
```

2. Let's examine the interaction between the decoder and rules so we can start using this for our own logs.

How it works...

Understanding how these messages are processed requires that we understand the path a log entry takes through the OSSEC analyzer. First, let's take a quick look at a flowchart, and then get into the specifics at each step. We'll look at an SSH-failed login message:

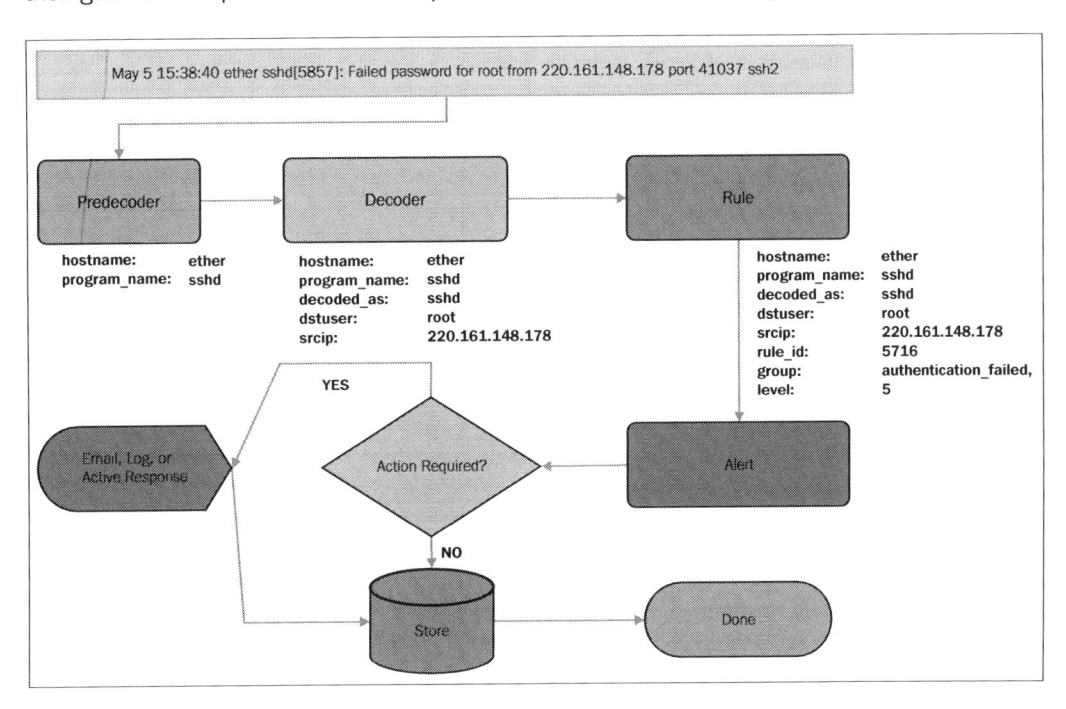

```
May 5 15:38:40 ether sshd[5857]: Failed password for root from 220.161.148.178 port 41037 ssh2
```

Predecoder
- hostname: ether
- program_name: sshd

Decoder
- hostname: ether
- program_name: sshd
- decoded_as: sshd
- dstuser: root
- srcip: 220.161.148.178

Rule
- hostname: ether
- program_name: sshd
- decoded_as: sshd
- dstuser: root
- srcip: 220.161.148.178
- rule_id: 5716
- group: authentication_failed,
- level: 5

Action Required?
- YES → Email, Log, or Active Response
- NO → Store

Alert → Done

The log message starts by passing through the predecoder to extract the program name, the hostname, timestamp, and deconstructs the log message without the metadata. The next step is to pass through the decoder to add context to the event. The rules are then parsed and a matching rule adds its data to the event and converts it to an alert. If there is an action to be taken (e-mail, log, or active response) for this event, it is dispatched. The details of the event are then tabulated in the OSSEC server for statistical reporting and aggregated analysis. The event has now finished processing. We need to understand how the selected decoders and rules interact to understand how OSSEC can protect our servers from SSH brute-force attacks.

Instant OSSEC Host-based Intrusion Detection

The SSH decoder starts off by anchoring itself to log messages with a `program_name` attribute starting with `sshd`. The `ssh-invfailed`, `ssh-failed`, and `ssh-error` decoders all anchor off the parent decoder; they're only loaded and evaluated if the SSHD decoder has matched. Each child rule uses a prematch operative that requires a simple regular expression to match before extraction is attempted.

Once that prematch is satisfied, the regex is called with an `offset` attribute set to `after_prematch`. Using this `offset` attribute, the string after the `prematch` string is handed to the `regex` attribute for extraction. Using the `offset` attribute shortens the string sent to the regular expression, eliminating duplication of matching operations.

For example, using our sample log message:

```
May   5 15:38:40 ether sshd[5857]: Failed password for root from 220.161.148.178 port 41037 ssh2
```

After the predecoder extracts the metadata, the decoders process the message as follows:

1. The `sshd` decoder matches the `program_name` attribute to the value `sshd`.
2. The `ssh-invfailed` decoder fails its prematch.
3. The `ssh-failed` decoder succeeds its prematch.
4. The string after the `prematch` string is sent through the decoder for extraction:

    ```
    root from 220.161.148.178 port 41037 ssh2
    ```

5. The `regex` element extracts two tokens through the use of grouping parentheses:

    ```
    'root', '220.161.148.178'
    ```

6. The `order` element tells the decoder about `user` and `srcip` respectively.
7. The log message is handed over to the rule engine for analysis as the decoder extracted data.

At this point, OSSEC is building an alert data structure for this message. The decoder uses its output to set the alert data for `srcip` and `user`. The `decoded_as` element is set to the parent of the decoder (`sshd` here).

The first rule (`5700`) serves as an anchor for the rest of the SSHD-based alerts. OSSEC uses this rule to form a tree of dependent rules. A parent rule referenced by other related rules helps optimize the path through the rules set. The `5700` rule matches successfully and the alert is set to level `0` and the `rule_id` attribute is set to `5700`.

The rule `5716` anchors to the parent rule using an `if_sid` attribute with a value `5700`. Since our sample message is from SSHD, the rule `5700` has matched and the next condition of the rule `5716` is evaluated. The message is checked to see if it starts with `Failed` or `error: PAM Authentication`. If the log entry matches, so that the alert level is updated to `5`, the `rule_id` attribute is updated to `5716` and the group is set to `authentication_failed`. After this point, no other rules looking for a rule ID of `5700` will match on this message.

The rule `5720` has a `frequency` attribute set to `6`. By setting the frequency, the analyzer will keep tabs on the number of times the rule is triggered in the next 6 minutes. We can use the `timeframe` attribute to change how long the analyzer tracks the number of times this rule is fired depending on our requirements.

The `if_matched_sid` attribute checks back 6 minutes to see if the `rule_id` value `5716` has been triggered 6 times. Remember, the rules are still being evaluated, so even though this rule is currently `5716`, there's no guarantee it will stay that way through the rules tree. During the first evaluation, the `if_matched_sid` attribute checks on the `rule_id` value `5716` and returns zero results.

We have an additional constraint of this `frequency/timeframe` attribute to check that the alert is from the same source IP using the `same_source_ip` attribute. This first message does not match `rule_id="5720"` this time, but it creates our counter for `rule_id="5720"` and source IP 220.161.148.178 at 1. Assuming these are the only rules we're using, the rule engine finishes, and an alert with the following data is created:

```
{
  'srcip'      : '220.161.148.178',
  'rule_id'    : 5716,
  'level'      : 5,
  'dstuser'    : 'root',
  'group'      : 'authentication_failed,',
  'decoded_as' : 'sshd'
}
```

You may notice that the way the log is parsed it will actually take seven failed login attempts in 6 minutes to trigger the `rule_id` value `5720`. On the seventh failed login attempt from 220.161.148.178, as any user, we'll finally hit the threshold on the `rule_id` value `5720`, and the alert will be rewritten as follows:

```
{
  'srcip'      : '220.161.148.178',
  'rule_id'    : 5720,
  'level'      : 10,
  'dstuser'    : 'mysql',
  'group'      : 'authentication_failed,authentication_failures,',
  'decoded_as' : 'sshd'
}
```

The important steps are that the `rule_id` attribute is replaced, as is the `level` attribute, and the `group` attribute has been appended.

Configuring the alerts (Simple)

The biggest failure of security software is the volume of unactionable alerts. Silencing alerts and investigating false positives robs an organization's valuable hours that it could use to enhance its security posture. OSSEC provides its users with options to fine-tune alerting to keep from becoming the boy who cried "Wolf!".

Getting ready

Armed with knowledge on how to write rules, we could just toggle alerting levels for all rules individually. This would be tedious, unless we used a generic catchall. However, that would destroy the granularity and precision of OSSEC analysis. It would be better to combine the two to maintain granularity and get e-mail alerting down to reasonable levels.

Every rule must set a level. The higher the level, the more severe the alert is considered. Alert levels are integers from 0 (ignore) to 15 (certain high-level security event). The official documentation has the definitive list of levels and their meanings and can be found via the following link:

http://www.ossec.net/doc/manual/rules-decoders/rule-levels.html

Rules can also append groups to the alert metadata. OSSEC ships with a number of defaults, and you're able to create your own. Here are a few interesting groups from the default rule set: invalid_login, authentication_success, authentication_failed, connection_attempt, and attacks.

Using just the level and group of an alert, you can configure a vast amount of alerts in a few lines of configuration.

How to do it...

Perform the following steps to configure alerts:

1. To do this, start with configuring the default log and the e-mail level for the alerts as follows:

   ```
   <alerts>
     <log_alert_level>1</log_alert_level>
     <email_alert_level>7</email_alert_level>
   </alerts>
   ```

2. To increase the default level to 9, change a single character in the ossec.conf file as follows:

   ```
   <alerts>
     <log_alert_level>1</log_alert_level>
     <email_alert_level>9</email_alert_level>
   </alerts>
   ```

3. OSSEC reports feature provides a flexible way to send condensed reports to give you daily insight into alerts that are interesting, though not actionable as individual events. To configure a report of successful logins, add this to your `ossec.conf` file:

[handwritten margin note: Set category for type of daily report.]

```
<reports>
  <category>authentication_success</category>
  <user type="relation">srcip</user>
  <title>OSSEC: Authentication Report</title>
  <email_to>security.alerts@example.com</email_to>
</reports>
```

How it works...

The e-mail alerting defaults on large networks may inundate administrators in the alerts for the log lines containing the word `error`. Log level 8 is reserved for first-time events, and you may not want to know the first time every administrator logs into every server in the network. Given that, we can reasonably adjust the level of the e-mail alerts to level 9 that is reserved for `Errors from Invalid Sources`.

This single-digit change may dramatically improve the volume of the alerts. You may wish to still receive periodic reports on the events not generating e-mails. The use of reports, alerts matching the source IDs, groups, or levels that are specified is summed up and broken down by key elements in the events: usernames, source IPs, event source hosts, levels, and groups.

Our sample report generates a daily report of authentication history for all installed and active OSSEC agents. This happens to be a common requirement for PCI-DSS, SOX, FISMA, or FERPA. The report will contain an aggregation of various categories; here's a sampling of some interesting data:

```
Report 'OSSEC: Authentication Report' completed.
------------------------------------------------
->Processed alerts: 1293
->Post-filtering alerts: 120
->First alert: 2013 May 10 02:00:02
->Last alert: 2013 May 10 22:05:25


Top entries for 'Source ip':
------------------------------------------------
192.168.0.1                                 |100
127.0.0.1                                   |19
1.2.3.4                                     |1
```

```
Top entries for 'Username':
-------------------------------------------------
compliance_scanner                              |100
root                                            |19
mallory                                         |1


Related entries for 'Username':
-------------------------------------------------
compliance_scanner                              |120
   srcip: '192.168.0.1'
root                                            |19
   srcip: '127.0.0.1'
mallory                                         |1
   srcip: '1.2.3.4'
```

This report uses the `relation` attribute to aggregate users by source IP to generate the last stanza of the report. It provides some clarity on the `Username` and `Source ip` sections to let us know where particular users originated. Each report requires an `email_to` attribute to be set to valid.

Another option that is often useful for very specific reports referencing a particular rule, or set of rules, is the `showlogs` option. Using this option, you can include a complete history of every log message that generated the alerts in the report. This option may generate large e-mails. To use it, add this to your report declaration:

```
<showlogs>yes</showlogs>
```

There's more...

These basic tweaks provide a lot of value, but there are a few additional tweaks we can use to clear up a few noisy alerts and integrate OSSEC with existing security workflows.

What is rule 1002 and why is it spamming me?

Even when toggling the default alert level, you will notice that they occasionally receive alerts below the threshold set in the `ossec.conf` file. This is because some rules override this setting by explicitly setting the e-mail alert flag. The "bad words" rule, ID 1002, is another example that overrides the default e-mail behavior. The rule is defined as follows:

```
<!-- Slightly modified for simplicity -->
<rule id="1002" level="2">
  <match>failure|error|attack|bad |illegal|denied|refused|unauthoriz
ed</match>
  <options>alert_by_email</options>
  <description>Unknown problem somewhere in the system.</description>
</rule>
```

This rule uses the `alert_by_email` option, which *always* alerts you regardless of the settings of the alert levels. Another set of rules that uses this override detects a restart of the OSSEC process. Rules that detect the start or stop of the OSSEC daemon also use this option to ensure that an e-mail alert is always sent. If you're not interested in these alerts, you can overwrite the rule and change its behavior using the `overwrite` attribute. This rule should be created in the `local_rules.xml` file as follows:

```xml
<rule id="1002" level="2" overwrite="yes">
  <match>failure|error|attack|bad |illegal|denied|refused|unauthorized</match>
  <options>no_email_alerts</options>
  <description>Unknown problem somewhere on the system (no_email_alert)</description>
</rule>
```

We need to redefine the rule with our modifications because the `overwrite` flag replaces the existing rule of that source ID entirely. The purpose of this method in creating a new source ID is so other rules dependent on this rule will not need to also be rewritten to accommodate the change. The downside is that if an improvement to the default rule is made in an OSSEC release, you will need to manually upgrade your `local_rules.xml` file with that update.

Playing nice with others

Once at a larger scale, it may become more useful to integrate OSSEC's alert logs into a larger **Security Information and Event Manager** (**SIEM**) such as Splunk or ArcSight. Luckily, OSSEC also supports the logging of events via syslog. Any event that OSSEC logs, which is level 1 and above by default, is also written to syslog. OSSEC supports multiple logging formats, including the following:

- `default`: This is the default full syslog output that can be used in hybrid mode
- `CEF`: This refers to ArcSight's Common Event Format
- `splunk`: This is the key-value output
- `json`: This refers to JSON-encoded events; it is most useful for LogStash or Graylog2

To enable one or more syslog outputs, you just need to declare the server and port values. OSSEC uses UDP for all syslog events as follows:

```xml
<syslog_output>
  <server>logserver.example.com</server>
  <port>514</port>
  <format>json</format>
</syslog_output>
```

This is plain syslog traffic and will not be encrypted. You can change the level for which a certain syslog server receives events by setting the log level in the syslog definition:

```
<syslog_output>
  <level>10</level>
  <server>critical-events.example.com</server>
  <port>514</port>
  <format>json</format>
</syslog_output>
```

You can also route certain events by rule group as follows:

```
<syslog_output>
  <group>authentication_success</group>
  <server>authenticationlogs.example.com</server>
  <port>514</port>
  <format>json</format>
</syslog_output>
```

Or, you can also route specific events by the source ID directly:

```
<syslog_output>
  <rule_id>1002</rule_id>
  <server>errors.example.com</server>
  <port>514</port>
  <format>json</format>
</syslog_output>
```

You may choose to completely disable e-mail alerting from OSSEC and use this syslog mechanism to work within your existing SIEM workflow.

File integrity monitoring (Simple)

File integrity monitoring (FIM) checks files and directories for changes. A number of commercial and open source solutions are available. OSSEC includes FIM as a part of its comprehensive solution to host-based intrusion detection. We'll briefly explore this feature and how to configure it.

Getting ready

File integrity monitoring looks at those attributes of a file that may indicate that its content has changed. These attributes include size, modification and creation times, one-way hashes of the contents of the file itself, and ownership and permissions of the file. Any change to one or more of these attributes triggers an alert. With OSSEC, we can customize the checks at a system-wide, per-directory, or even per-file level.

Instant OSSEC Host-based Intrusion Detection

How to do it...

We're going to tune the default configuration to monitor additional directories, to always alert on file changes, and to configure the scanning to occur when our systems aren't under heavy load.

1. Configure the `syscheck` section of the `ossec.conf` file as follows:

```xml
<syscheck>
    <!-- Alert Enhancements -->
    <auto_ignore>no</auto_ignore>
    <alert_new_files>yes</alert_new_files>

    <!-- Better Scheduling -->
    <scan_on_start>no</scan_on_start>
    <scan_time>3am</scan_time>
    <frequency>82800</frequency>

    <!-- Directories to check -->
    <directories check_all="yes" realtime="yes">/etc</directories>
    <directories check_all="yes">/usr/bin,/usr/sbin</directories>
    <directories check_all="yes">/bin,/sbin</directories>
    <directories check_all="yes">/usr/local/bin</directories>
    <directories check_all="yes" restrict="authorized_keys">/root/.ssh</directories>

    <!-- Files/directories to ignore -->
    <ignore>/etc/mtab</ignore>
    <ignore>/etc/hosts.deny</ignore>
    <ignore>/etc/mail/statistics</ignore>
    <ignore>/etc/random-seed</ignore>
    <ignore>/etc/adjtime</ignore>
    <ignore>/etc/httpd/logs</ignore>
    <ignore>/etc/prelink.cache</ignore>
</syscheck>
```

2. Once you have finished configuring this section, restart OSSEC.

How it works...

After a few a days of running the default configuration, you may notice that the alarm volume drops off dramatically from the FIM. The default configuration automatically ignores any file that changes beyond the third change, assuming the changes are a part of the normal operation. While this helps with the volume of the alerts, it may not satisfy your compliance requirements. To receive these alerts, we need to disable the `auto_ignore` feature of `syscheck` daemon by setting it to no.

Instant OSSEC Host-based Intrusion Detection

When the `syscheck` daemon detects a new file, it silently creates an entry using this new file's attributes as the baseline. A file's initial state is considered clean and only changes to that state will trigger alerts. If you wish to receive notifications when a file is added to a directory, you may tell OSSEC to notify you by setting `alert_new_files` to `yes`.

Now that we have enabled comprehensive alerting on changes to files and directories, we can start to fine-tune the performance of the `syscheck` daemon. By default, a restart of OSSEC' `syscheck` daemon starts a scan of all the directories being monitored. This may not be ideal if you need to restart OSSEC for configuration changes in the middle of your peak utilization. To be safe, we disable the startup scan by setting `scan_on_start` to `no`.

Now the scans will schedule in accordance with the values defined by our `frequency` attribute, ignoring daemon restarts. You may have noticed that there has been a possible impact on the performance of this system. Disks just aren't as fast as the rest of our system components. If we're doing scans of directories with a substantially large number and/or size, it's going to impact the performance of the rest of the system. This is true of any FIM solution and not just OSSEC.

To avoid these performance penalties, OSSEC has an option of utilizing the **inotify** system to check only those files that change. In our directories definition, we set the `realtime` attribute to `yes`, and on systems supporting inotify, checks will automatically run when the file or directory is updated.

This means we can relax our scanner further and schedule the full scan to run at a low usage time during the day. We configured `syscheck` to start scans at 3 A.M., after a minimum of 23 hours (82,800 seconds) since the last scan. For the `/etc`, `/usr/bin` and `/usr/sbin` directories, we enable the `realtime` notifications if they are supported on the host system. File modifications in these directories will be scanned as they occur at 3 A.M. everyday. For the remaining directories, the `realtime` option hasn't been enabled, so they will only be scanned once per day at 3 A.M.

Play with these settings to get adequate coverage without imposing a performance penalty on your network or systems.

There's more...

Working with the OSSEC FIM implementation is nice given how flexible it is. It even has extended capabilities for Windows and hooks for Linux systems using prelinking.

Monitoring the Windows registry

OSSEC's FIM module also supports the monitoring of the Windows registry. On a Windows systems, you may want to be notified anytime the startup items are changed:

```xml
<syscheck>
    <!-- scheduling and directories would go here -->
    <windows_registry>HKEY_LOCAL_MACHINE\System\CurrentControlSet\Services</windows_registry>
    <windows_registry>HKEY_LOCAL_MACHINE\Software\Microsoft\Windows\CurrentVersion\RunServicesOnce</windows_registry>
    <windows_registry>HKEY_LOCAL_MACHINE\Software\Microsoft\Windows\CurrentVersion\RunServices</windows_registry>
    <!-- Repeat for all interesting registry keys -->
</syscheck>
```

You could also specify a root node to monitor and use it with the `registry_ignore` declarations to enable more comprehensive monitoring of the Windows registry.

Working with prelinking

On some Linux systems, **prelinking** is enabled by default. Prelinking decreases application startup time but makes changes to the binary file. These changes trigger alerts in any FIM solution. To cut down on alerting due to prelinking, OSSEC added the ability to send the binary files through the prelink verification process. This process is expensive, but if you are seeing a high volume of alerts caused by prelinking, you can add this to the `syscheck` section of your `ossec.conf` file:

```xml
<prefilter_cmd>/usr/sbin/prelink -y</prefilter_cmd>
```

Monitoring command output (Intermediate)

OSSEC can monitor more than just logfiles; it can also monitor the output of commands. OSSEC can leverage its log analysis engine using rules and decoders to alert when a command outputs a certain string. OSSEC can also leverage its file integrity monitoring facilities to alert when the output of a command changes from the previous run. We'll look at a few examples where this might be useful.

Getting ready

OSSEC treats command output as log entries. OSSEC has two options for command monitoring: `command` and `full_command`. The difference is how OSSEC handles the output. When using the `command` variation, every line of output is treated as an individual log entry and analyzed independently. When using the `full_command` variation, the entire output is regarded as a single log entry.

Instant OSSEC Host-based Intrusion Detection

OSSEC's internal rules match the command output using the source ID `530` and prefix each log entry with the alias or command that is run as follows:

`ossec: output: 'df -h' ...`

`ossec: output: 'my-command-alias' ...`

We'll use this knowledge to write rules to handle the output of two commands: one to monitor changes to listening ports with `netstat` and another to monitor disk usage with `df`.

How to do it...

1. To enable command monitoring in OSSEC, configure the commands as `localfile` entries in the `ossec.conf` file:

   ```
   <!-- Commands to Monitor -->
   <localfile>
     <log_format>command</log_format>
     <command>df -l -x tmpfs |grep -v '^Filesystem'|awk '{print $1 " mounted as " $6 " usage is " $5 }'</command>
     <alias>disk-usage</alias>
     <frequency>3600</frequency>
   </localfile>

   <localfile>
     <log_format>full_command</log_format>
     <command>netstat -nltu</command>
     <alias>netstat-listening</alias>
     <frequency>600</frequency>
   </localfile>
   ```

2. Once the commands are declared, put some rules together in your `local_rules.xml` file to configure alerting:

   ```
   <rule id="100100" level="2">
     <if_sid>530</if_sid>
     <match>ossec: output: 'disk-usage'</match>
     <group>system_availability,</group>
   </rule>

   <rule id="100101" level="12">
     <if_sid>100100</if_sid>
     <regex>usage is 9\d</regex>
     <description>Critically high disk usage.</description>
   </rule>
   ```

```xml
<rule id="100102" level="13">
  <if_sid>100100</if_sid>
  <match>usage is 100</match>
  <options>alert_by_email</options>
  <description>Disk is full, availability in jeopardy.</description>
</rule>
```

3. For the listening ports' `netstat` command, handle the entire output as a single entity, alerting users in case of any changes:

```xml
<rule id="100200" level="2">
  <if_sid>530</if_sid>
  <match>ossec: output: 'netstat-listening'</match>
  <check_diff/>
  <options>alert_by_email</options>
  <group>network_services,</group>
</rule>
```

With this rule configured, if the listening ports change, we'll receive an e-mail informing us of the current and previous output of the `netstat` command.

How it works...

The commands are defined in the `ossec.conf` file, similar to logfiles, except they require a `command` attribute to tell OSSEC what command and arguments to execute. They use the `log_format` element having value as the `command` or `full_command` variation so OSSEC knows how to execute the command and how to handle the output. We're using an alias for these declarations so the rules will be easier to write.

In both our command declarations, we used command pipes, |, to either exclude or format the output of our commands to make alerts more relevant. The `df` example uses `awk` to completely rewrite the output of the `df` command; this makes it easier to read and match using OSSEC's regex/match capabilities. Let's break it down:

```
df -l -x tmpfs |grep -v '^Filesystem'|awk '{print $1 " mounted as " $6 " usage is " $5 }'
```

We use the `df` command to list the capacity and usage of our locally mounted filesystems. We skip the nonlocally mounted filesystems because if an NFS volume fills up, it will alert potentially every server in our infrastructure. We're also excluding the shared memory filesystem, `tmpfs`. The output of this command on my server is as follows:

```
$ df -l -x tmpfs
Filesystem     1K-blocks     Used   Available  Use%  Mounted on
/dev/xvda      20421052   9134172   10458508   47%   /
/dev/xvdc      16513960   7980512    7694588   51%   /home
```

Since we're using the `command` option, each line is treated as its own log entry. If this is the case, the header to the `df` command isn't really worth analyzing, so we remove it using `grep -v '^Filesystem'` to exclude the lines starting with the word `'Filesystem'`.

```
$ df -l -x tmpfs |grep -v '^Filesystem'
/dev/xvda        20421052   9134172   10458508   47% /
/dev/xvdc        16513960   7980512    7694588   51% /home
```

The output is usable, but it's not as simple as it could be. So using `awk` we rewrite each line by printing the first word ($1), " mounted as ", the sixth word ($6), " usage is ", and finally the fifth word ($5). The `awk` command's defaults interpret the white space as word separators.

```
$ df -l -x tmpfs |grep -v '^Filesystem'\
>       |awk '{print $1 " mounted as " $6 " usage is " $5 }'
/dev/xvda mounted as / usage is 47%
/dev/xvdc mounted as /home usage is 51%
```

Using this format, it's easier to write rules and easier for administrators receiving alerts to understand what they mean. We can then start writing rules to notify administrators as follows:

```
<rule id="100100" level="2">
  <if_sid>530</if_sid>
  <match>ossec: output: 'disk-usage'</match>
  <group>system_availability,</group>
</rule>
```

The first rule for the `disk-usage` command anchors the rest of the rules as their parent. It also appends the `system_availability` group to the alert. We could use this group to route alerts to different e-mails, active responses, or look at aggregates. The next rule that we'll write looks at 90 to 99 percent disk usage:

```
<rule id="100101" level="12">
  <if_sid>100100</if_sid>
  <regex>usage is 9\d</regex>
  <description>Critically high disk usage.</description>
</rule>
```

This rule will alert a high-importance event at level `12`. To match this, the rule anchors to the rule `100100` with the `if_sid` declaration. The `regex` element is used to look for `usage is 9` followed by the other digit `\d`—when the usage is 90 to 99 percent. Once the disk goes to 100 percent, this rule will stop matching; so, we'll need another rule to handle this special case:

```
<rule id="100102" level="13">
  <if_sid>100100</if_sid>
  <match>usage is 100</match>
  <options>alert_by_email</options>
  <description>Disk is full, availability in jeopardy.</description>
</rule>
```

This rule again anchors itself to the parent rule, `100100`. We can't have a disk at 101 percent usage or higher so we look for 100 percent only. The alert level is raised to `13` (unusual error), and we explicitly set the `alert_by_email` option so we can be assured that this alert will always generate an e-mail regardless of our other e-mail and report settings.

Our next command monitors the listening of the TCP and UDP ports using `netstat`.

```
netstat -nltu
```

This calls the `netstat` command with the following options: do not look up hostnames (`-n`), show only listening sockets (`-l`), show TCP sockets (`-t`), and show UDP sockets (`-u`).

To accomplish our goal, it's not necessary to transform or decode the output of the `netstat` command. A simple difference between the current and previous run is sufficient. We can achieve this with a single rule:

```
<rule id="100200" level="2">
  <if_sid>530</if_sid>
  <match>ossec: output: 'netstat-listening'</match>
  <check_diff/>
  <options>alert_by_email</options>
  <group>network_services,</group>
</rule>
```

We check the source ID `530`, the source ID for the command output, and the match using the alias for the command `netstat-listening`. We add the `network_services` group to the alerts. To check for differences, you need only specify the `check_diff` attribute to the rule. The alert level is `2` (system information), but we really want to know about these events so we set the `alert_by_email` flag on the alert.

Detecting rootkits and anomalies (Simple)

OSSEC ships with a rootkit detection module that looks specifically for traces of rootkits, malware, and Trojans on configured systems. This recipe looks briefly at configuring the `rootcheck` module.

Getting ready

The OSSEC `syscheck` daemon runs the rootkit module. There are a few components of the rootkit detection module, all configurable individually. They are as follows:

- **File detection**: This component looks for malicious files at known locations
- **/dev check**: This component looks in `/dev` for executable files
- **PID check**: This component looks for processes hidden from `ps`
- **Port check**: This component looks for open ports hidden from `netstat`

Instant OSSEC Host-based Intrusion Detection

- **Interface check**: This component looks for an interface in promiscuous mode
- **System scan**: This component looks for anomalies in the filesystem, that is, for bad permissions and strange SUID (set user ID) files
- **Policy checks**: This component looks for weird items in files; its submodules are as follows:
    - **Trojans check**: This module looks for well-known Trojans on the system
    - **Windows malware**: This module looks for well-known malware
    - **Windows application**: This module looks for bad applications
    - **System audit**: This module looks for bad configurations that would be a violation of the best practices according to industry standards

Some of these checks, like the interface check, are really simple and quick while others like the policy check can be quite resource intensive.

How to do it...

Here are some guidelines for detecting rootkits and anomalies:

1. Check OSSEC's default configuration of the `rootcheck` daemon in `ossec.conf`:

   ```
   <rootcheck>
       <rootkit_files>/var/ossec/etc/shared/rootkit_files.txt</rootkit_files>
       <rootkit_trojans>/var/ossec/etc/shared/rootkit_trojans.txt</rootkit_trojans>
   </rootcheck>
   ```

2. To completely disable the rootkit module, change the `rootcheck` section to the following:

   ```
   <rootcheck>
       <disabled>yes</disabled>
   </rootcheck>
   ```

3. Disabling the rootkit detection module isn't ideal, but there are some exceptional cases we might need to address. A better configuration for a CPU-bound system is as follows:

   ```
   <rootcheck>
       <frequency>172800</frequency>

       <!-- Disable CPU heavy checks due to network connections -->
       <check_ports>no</check_ports>
       <rootkit_files>/var/ossec/etc/shared/rootkit_files.txt</rootkit_files>
   ```

```
        <rootkit_trojans>/var/ossec/etc/shared/rootkit_trojans.txt</
        rootkit_trojans>
    </rootcheck>
```

4. If we had a disk-bound system, it might be wise to disable the intensive disk checks as follows:

```
<rootcheck>
    <frequency>172800</frequency>

    <!-- Disable high disk IO Checks -->
    <check_policy>no</check_policy>
    <check_sys>no</check_sys>
    <rootkit_files>/var/ossec/etc/shared/rootkit_files.txt</
    rootkit_files>
    <rootkit_trojans>/var/ossec/etc/shared/rootkit_trojans.txt</
    rootkit_trojans>
</rootcheck>
```

How it works...

OSSEC's default configuration enables all the rootkit checks. With the rest of the modules running, we adjust the `frequency` attribute from the default value of every 20 hours to every 48 hours.

There are a few heavy checks that are enabled depending on your system profiles. On systems that use network filesystems (NFS), the `rootcheck` daemon may cause performance problems while running checks that read data from the filesystem.

The `check_policy` attribute actually controls the policy checks, including the `trojans`, `winmalware`, `winapps`, `unixaudit`, and `winaudit` checks. These checks inspect the contents of files on the filesystem, looking for misconfiguration. You can disable one or more of these checks individually, but as they scan the same places, it's best to disable the entire set.

The system scan can also lead to high-disk input/output and degrade system performance, though it's very rare. We can disable it by setting `check_sys` to `no` in the `rootcheck` section as we previously saw. This check isn't opening a lot of files but is using the `stat` system call to look at permissions. You may have guessed that this is more expensive on network filesystems but also on systems with a large number of files.

For systems that have a large number of network connections open at the same time, you may find that the port check component can take a lot of CPU. Port check uses `netstat` to determine either currently open ports or closed ports with live connections. On systems with several thousand concurrent, open connections, this check can actually impact production performance. You can disable this check by setting `check_ports` to `no` in the `rootcheck` section.

Instant OSSEC Host-based Intrusion Detection

There may be an overlap where you have both a large number of connections as well as network-mounted filesystems. Disabling individual checks is not exclusive, so you can disable as many as you need to get the performance to reasonable levels.

There's more...

The `rootcheck` daemon can be configured to do more precise or more sweeping scans.

Auditing your systems

The `rootcheck` module uses a file configuration syntax that can and has been extended to provide the system audit capability. It provides a notation for "if this directory contains an executable" and "if this file contains this line". It can audit the configuration of critical services and identify violations of corporate or security policy.

Increasing paranoia

There are some servers that keep administrators up at night. If these systems have resources to spare, you can enable a "paranoid" mode on the `rootcheck` module. This setting does away with the notion of "look in well-known places for bad things" and enables "look everywhere on the system for bad things". While this sounds spectacular, it is very resource intensive and should be used only where necessary.

To enable the "paranoid" mode, configure the `rootcheck` module as follows:

```
<rootcheck>
    <!-- Enable Scanning of ALL THE THINGS! -->
    <scanall>yes</scanall>
     <frequency>86400</frequency>
    <!-- etc, .. -->
</rootcheck>
```

I recommend setting a custom `frequency` attribute when you enable `scanall`, if only to make yourself aware. Use periods that are common to monitoring systems: days, weeks, or months. The default of 20 hours can drive administrators insane trying to track down why the server is under high load at seemingly random times on their graphs.

Introducing active response (Intermediate)

A standout feature of OSSEC is its active response module. Active response allows commands to be executed based on the triggering of a rule. It provides these commands with network, user, and file information from the rules that tripped the active response. With the active response system, you can provide targeted protection to your network. Using this mechanism, it is possible to implement the functionality of the popular **Fail2Ban SSH** brute-force protection using OSSEC.

Getting ready

In order to implement active response, you will need to know how active response commands are called. The `firewall-drop.sh` script ships with OSSEC implementing the locking and logging feature, and also works on most Linux/BSD systems. We'll take a look at an incredibly distilled version of the script to understand how active response works:

```sh
#!/bin/sh
#
ACTION=$1
SRCIP=$3

if [ "$ACTION" == "add"]; then
    /usr/sbin/iptables -I FORWARD -s $SRCIP -j DROP
    /usr/sbin/iptables -I INPUT -s $SRCIP -j DROP
elif [ "$ACTION" == "delete"]; then
    /usr/sbin/iptables -D FORWARD -s $SRCIP -j DROP
    /usr/sbin/iptables -D INPUT -s $SRCIP -j DROP
else
    echo "invalid action, specific add or delete";
    exit 1;
fi;
```

Our distilled `firewall-drop.sh` script is a simple shell script that receives the arguments starting with `$1` from the command-line call. It doesn't implement any error-checking mechanism and assumes the host system is a Linux-based distribution with the `iptables` binary in `/usr/sbin/iptables`. It checks the `$1` parameter for the action, which will be either add or delete, and executes the `iptables` commands to add or remove the IP for the appropriate tables.

The trickiest part of the script is knowing what each positional parameter represents. Here's a simple breakdown for Linux/BSD shell scripting:

Position	Shell variable	Description
1	$1	Action: add or delete
2	$2	Event: User or hyphen (-) if empty
3	$3	Event: Source IP or hyphen (-) if empty
4	$4	Event ID (unique per event)
5	$5	Event rule ID or source ID
6	$6	Event information: This may contain the agent name, host, or filename based on the context

Instant OSSEC Host-based Intrusion Detection

Using these variables, you could create your own active responses to integrate with your existing network and host security infrastructures.

How to do it...

Perform the following steps to introduce the active response module:

1. OSSEC ships with a few active response commands included. Configure OSSEC with active response and enable the `firewall-drop` command; you should now have a `command` attribute set up in the `ossec.conf` file already, as follows:

```
<command>
    <name>firewall-drop</name>
    <executable>firewall-drop.sh</executable>
    <expect>srcip</expect>
    <timeout_allowed>yes</timeout_allowed>
</command>
```

2. To implement the Fail2Ban functionality, configure the active response a bit more than the stock `ossec.conf` file:

```
<active-response>
    <command>firewall-drop</command>
    <location>local</location>
    <rules_id>5551,5712,5720,31151</rules_id>
    <timeout>600</timeout>
    <repeated_offenders>600,3600,86400</repeated_offenders>
</active-response>
```

How it works...

When setting up commands, OSSEC is configured to look for the `firewall-drop.sh` script in the `/var/ossec/active-response/bin` directory. We declared the command to expect a source IP, so events dispatching this command without a valid source IP will be ignored. A timeout is allowed for active responses that call this command, allowing the pruning of unnecessary firewall rules by setting `timeout_allowed` to `yes`.

We add an `active-response` element to run the `firewall-drop` command. The location in this case is the local agent generating the alarm, but we could simply say "all" or specify a specific agent ID where the command needs to be run.

Adding and deleting firewall rules from production systems should be something that's *very* deliberate and specific. We configure the response to be fired on the following rules: `5551`, `5712`, `5720`, and `31151`. This is a selection of rules that indicates SSH brute-force probes/attacks. This is much more predictable than using groups or levels as sources of events.

A `timeout` value of `600` seconds is set for this active response. When this active response fires the first time, the script will be called with the `action` parameter set to `add`. Ten minutes later, OSSEC will re-run the script with the same parameters, only this time modifying the `action` parameter to `delete`.

Using the `repeat_offenders` parameter, we can adjust this timeout based on how frequently a particular source IP trips this active response. The first two timeouts are 10 minutes, the third time that the same IP trips the alert it moves into blocking mode for an hour, and for the fourth and for all subsequent times, the IP is blocked for 24 hours.

Active response can be configured to run anywhere on the network, so there's really no limit to how interesting your responses can be. There's also nothing preventing you from leveraging the active response system to assist you in tracking events. You could easily create a simple shell script to integrate OSSEC alerting directly into a ticketing system, such as JIRA, RTIR, or Remedy.

Verifying alerts with active response (Advanced)

As a deployment of OSSEC expands and matures, so does the volume of alerts. Normal activities, such as system packages updates, updates to critical configuration files, and users' interaction with those systems, generate alerts. This section will explore the possibility of using active response to assist with the verification of changes to a user's list of scheduled tasks (crontab).

Getting ready

Shortly after enabling OSSEC on my network, I began receiving alerts for "normal" changes to the environment. Our configuration management software, **Puppet**, was generating alerts by updating the crontab of the root user. When Puppet manages a user's crontab, it prepends a header to the file as follows:

```
# HEADER: This file was autogenerated at 2013-03-01 13:30:53 +0100 by puppet.
```

Implementing a script to check Puppet's modification time against the crontab modification time isn't difficult. We just need to know how to leverage the entire OSSEC infrastructure.

Unfortunately, OSSEC does not provide a decoder to extract fields from crontab log messages. Luckily, we can easily extend the decoders! We'll add a small decoder to handle crontab messages and extract the username.

Instant OSSEC Host-based Intrusion Detection

How to do it...

To verify alerts with active response, perform the following steps:

1. Set up decoders for our crontab log entries and our new logging target `ossec-ar-verify`. Then place them in the `/var/ossec/etc/decoders.d` directory and tell OSSEC to look there for our custom decoders. Also, add the `command` and `active-response` elements to the `ossec.conf` files:

   ```
   <command>
     <name>ossec-ar-verify-crontab</name>
     <executable>ossec-ar-verify-crontab.sh</executable>
     <expect>username</expect>
     <timeout_allowed>no</timeout_allowed>
   </command>
   <active-response>
     <command>ossec-ar-verify-crontab</command>
     <location>local</location>
     <rules_id>106001</rules_id>
   </active-response>
   <rules>
     <!-- OSSEC Decoders -->
     <decoder>etc/decoder.xml</decoder>
     <!-- Load my custom decoders -->
     <decoder_dir>etc/decoders.d</decoder_dir>
     <!-- Rest of rules -->
   </rules>
   ```

2. Next, set up the `crontab.xml` decoder:

   ```
   <decoder name="crontab">
     <program_name>crontab</program_name>
   </decoder>

   <decoder name="crontab-user">
     <parent>crontab</parent>
     <regex>^\(((\S+)\) </regex>
     <order>user</order>
   </decoder>
   ```

3. After that, set up the `ossec-ar-verify.xml` decoder:

   ```
   <decoder name="ossec-ar-verify">
     <program_name>ossec-ar-verify</program_name>
   </decoder>
   ```

Instant OSSEC Host-based Intrusion Detection

```xml
<decoder name="ossec-ar-verify-crontab">
  <parent>ossec-ar-verify</parent>
  <prematch>^crontab </prematch>
  <regex offset="after_prematch">^(\S+)</regex>
  <order>user</order>
</decoder>
```

4. Then define the rules to handle the triggering of the active response and then interpret the results in our `local_rules.xml` file:

```xml
<rule id="106001" level="1">
  <if_sid>2833</if_sid>
  <options>no_email_alert</options>
  <description>Verify the crontab modification</description>
</rule>
<rule id="107000" level="11">
  <decoded_as>ossec-ar-verify</decoded_as>
  <description>OSSEC ActiveResponse Verification</description>
  <group>verified,</group>
</rule>
<rule id="107001" level="12">
  <if_sid>107000</if_sid>
  <match>^crontab </match>
  <options>alert_by_email</options>
  <description>Verified: Crontab changed outside of Puppet</description>
  <group>oob_change,scheduled_tasks</group>
</rule>
```

5. Also, distribute a Perl script to handle your date math with a wrapper shell script. The wrapper script `ossec-ar-verify.sh` referenced in our command declaration is as follows:

```sh
#!/bin/sh

USER=$2
CRONTAB="/var/spool/cron/$USER"

if [ -f "$CRONTAB" ]; then
    /usr/local/bin/ossec-ar-verify-crontab.pl $CRONTAB
    rc=$?

    if [ "$rc" != "0" ]; then
        logger -t ossec-ar-verify "crontab $USER change outside Puppet"
    fi
fi
```

Instant OSSEC Host-based Intrusion Detection

How it works...

OSSEC includes the rule `2833` to identify when the root's crontab changes. We need to take action on this alert and generate another more serious alert if the validation against Puppet fails. The steps to verify the alert are as follows:

1. If the rule `2833` fires, silence it.
2. Run an active response command on the agent generating the alert.
3. If validation fails, inform OSSEC via syslog.
4. OSSEC should understand the new notification and alert via e-mail.

For step 1, rule `2833` uses the `alert_by_email` option to always send an e-mail regardless of the level of the alert. Since we're going to be verifying this alert, we need to disable that e-mail. The best way to do this is to create a new rule (`100601`) in our `local_rules.xml` file to turn off the e-mail alert.

To enable the active response required in step 2, we need three things: a script to run, a `command` declaration in the `ossec.conf` file, and an `active-response` declaration in `ossec.conf`. In simple words, the script we're calling is a wrapper around another script that checks the file modification time of the crontab file against the date of the header provided by Puppet. If they vary by more than 1 minute, the script exits with an error; if the times match, the script exits successfully. Our wrapper script uses these exit codes to determine whether or not to generate a new syslog message by calling the logger program. If the dates match, no message is generated; if they don't, the following command is called:

```
logger -t ossec-ar-verify "crontab root changed outside puppet"
```

This may be the first of many verification scripts, so we create a namespace for this purpose; `ossec-ar-verify` is descriptive and succinct. We name this command `ossec-ar-verify-crontab` with an absolute path of `/var/ossec/active-response/bin/ossec-ar-verify-crontab.sh`. This script requires a username to be set so we know whose crontab to verify. Since it's only being run once per alert, there's no need to use the timeout features; so we've disabled them. Next we have to configure the `active-response` element to use this command.

We created a child of rule 2833, and the source ID of that new rule is `106001`. This script needs to be run at the source of the event, so we configure the location of this active response to be `local`. The command variation is set to `ossec-ar-verify-crontab`.

We need events to pass a username to the active response, but OSSEC doesn't ship with a decoder for crontab log messages. Without it, our active response would never fire and we'd silently discard all these messages. We create a `crontab.xml` decoder file and place it in the `/var/ossec/etc/decoder.d` directory we configured to be loaded in the `ossec.conf` file. This decoder extracts the username from the crontab log messages to pass to the active response.

For step 3, we're going to simply send a new log message via syslog if the verification fails, which will look similar to the following:

```
Jun  2 12:57:38 host ossec-ar-verify[640]: crontab changed outside Puppet
```

We create an `ossec-ar-verify.xml` file in our `/var/ossec/etc/decoder.d` directory to extract fields from messages to our new syslog target `ossec-ar-verify`. The decoder parent will be named `ossec-ar-verify`, so we can use the high-speed `decoded_as` attribute for anchoring rules.

The two decoders work together to set the `decoded_as` attribute in the event and extract the `user` attribute from the crontab alerts. The `regex` attribute in our second decoder line extracts the first word after the `prematch` element (crontab in our example). The `order` element assigns names to the variable extracted using grouping parentheses. We're only extracting a single value named `user`.

If the modification times don't match, step 4 of our model is triggered by our log messages. We create a rule `107000` to anchor any current and future `ossec-ar-verify` messages; this rule also appends a `verified` group to the alert that we can use for reporting. The rule `107001` matches messages starting with the word `crontab`. It sets the `alert_by_email` option to notify the administrators. It also appends the `oob_change` (out of band change) and `scheduled_tasks` groups to the alert for reporting.

Hopefully, this example will make you wonder, "Couldn't I extend this same pattern to verify file checksum changes against our package manager and/or configuration engine?". Yes! Given the scriptability of the active response system, you are not limited by vendor lock-in and can incorporate data sources for verification from anywhere in your organization. You are limited only by your own creativity!

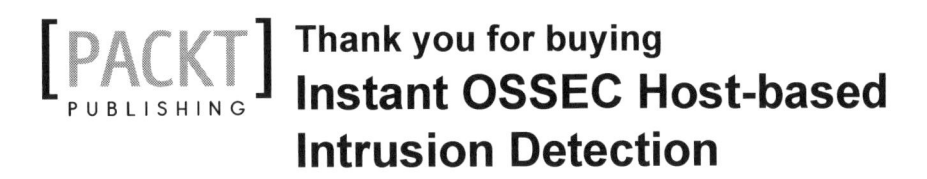

Thank you for buying
Instant OSSEC Host-based Intrusion Detection

About Packt Publishing

Packt, pronounced 'packed', published its first book "*Mastering phpMyAdmin for Effective MySQL Management*" in April 2004 and subsequently continued to specialize in publishing highly focused books on specific technologies and solutions.

Our books and publications share the experiences of your fellow IT professionals in adapting and customizing today's systems, applications, and frameworks. Our solution based books give you the knowledge and power to customize the software and technologies you're using to get the job done. Packt books are more specific and less general than the IT books you have seen in the past. Our unique business model allows us to bring you more focused information, giving you more of what you need to know, and less of what you don't.

Packt is a modern, yet unique publishing company, which focuses on producing quality, cutting-edge books for communities of developers, administrators, and newbies alike. For more information, please visit our website: www.packtpub.com.

Writing for Packt

We welcome all inquiries from people who are interested in authoring. Book proposals should be sent to author@packtpub.com. If your book idea is still at an early stage and you would like to discuss it first before writing a formal book proposal, contact us; one of our commissioning editors will get in touch with you.

We're not just looking for published authors; if you have strong technical skills but no writing experience, our experienced editors can help you develop a writing career, or simply get some additional reward for your expertise.

Instant Citrix XenDesktop 5 Starter

ISBN: 978-1-78217-002-0   Paperback: 66 pages

Your step-by-step guide to building a full-fledged XenDesktop infrastructure from scratch

1. Learn something new in an Instant! A short, fast, focused guide delivering immediate results.
2. Know how to install XenDesktop, integrate it with PVS and build streamed and pooled desktops
3. Learn how to build provisioning servers, capture VHD files, and configure streaming

Instant Spring Security Starter

ISBN: 978-1-78216-883-6   Paperback: 70 pages

Learn the fundamentals of web authentication and authorization using Spring Security

1. Learn something new in an Instant! A short, fast, focused guide delivering immediate results
2. Learn basic login/password and two-phase authentication
3. Secure access all the way from frontend to backend
4. Learn about the available security models, SPEL, and pragmatic considerations

Please check **www.PacktPub.com** for information on our titles

[PACKT] PUBLISHING

BackTrack - Testing Wireless Network Security

ISBN: 978-1-78216-406-7   Paperback: 108 pages

Secure your wireless networks against attacks, hacks, and intruders with this step-by-step guide

1. Make your wireless networks bulletproof
2. Easily secure your network from intruders
3. See how the hackers do it and learn how to defend yourself

Metasploit Penetration Testing Cookbook

ISBN: 978-1-84951-742-3   Paperback: 268 pages

Over 70 recipes to master the most widely used penetration testing framework

1. More than 80 recipes/practicaltasks that will escalate the reader's knowledge from beginner to an advanced level
2. Special focus on the latest operating systems, exploits, and penetration testing techniques
3. Detailed analysis of third party tools based on the Metasploit framework to enhance the penetration testing experience

Please check www.PacktPub.com for information on our titles